Fantasy of Loving the Fantasy

fantasy
of loving *the*
fantasy

poems

Jennifer Funk

BULL★CITY
PRESS

Durham, NC

Library of Congress Cataloging-in-Publication Data

Names: Funk, Jennifer, 1985- author.
Title: Fantasy of loving the fantasy : poems / Jennifer Funk.
Other titles: Fantasy of loving the fantasy (Compilation)
Description: Durham, NC : Bull City Press, [2023] Identifiers:
LCCN 2022025359 (print) | LCCN 2022025360 (ebook) | ISBN
9781949344349 (paperback) | ISBN 9781949344387 (ebook)
Subjects: LCGFT: Poetry.
Classification: LCC PS3606.U653 F36 2023 (print) |
LCC PS3606.U653 (ebook) | DDC 811/.6--dc23/eng/20230601
LC record available at https://lccn.loc.gov/2022025359
LC ebook record available at https://lccn.loc.gov/2022025360

Published in the United States of America

Cover art: *Sleep Elevations XIV*, Maia Flore
Book design: Spock and Associates

Published by BULL CITY PRESS
1217 Odyssey Drive
Durham, NC 27713
www.BullCityPress.com

Table of Contents

for my mother

Fantasy of Losing My Suburban Cool

Don't look at me like you've just come in from the fields
and aren't I thankful you've arrived. Like all the men
who open their wallets easily, you don't know
what anything costs. I see a man sometimes
and want to ruin his life just because
I have nothing better to do. Look at the crest
of my lips. I have sunk more than one ship
with this mouth. Perhaps you don't merit
my attention, but you need it: a good shake
of the old snow globe. How ever to begin?
I would rip the doors of your kitchen cabinets
clean off their hinges, smash every glass jar
of cereal and rice and unground coffee
onto your immaculate tile, seize the curtains
from the windows, and break over my knee
every picture in a frame. I would wrest open every window
and ribbon every screen with your best butcher knife
so that when I make for the sports gear—the skis and poles
and rackets and lacrosse sticks—I'd have a ready portal
for them all. I'd stake each one into the emerald
glory of your lawn and with a box of matches
I'd swiped from your very own mantel, I'm no mere
country mouse, I'd light the tip of every one on fire, and not for love
and just for sport, I'd sit across the street and toast my work
as the sun slips down, and you can bet the sky tonight
will be a riot of color in my honor.

Make Me Familiar

In August, still early, before night has yielded fully,
when the air still prickles the skin, and the sky is bluesy pink
like berries pressed to bursting in a bowl, you can find yourself,

or I, I can find myself, creature of terminal haste, creature
ever mid-stride, reconsidering the world in the middle of the road.
It's early. There are no cars. Say there was never any bang,

say there was no great cosmic heave, say the world began
as some mornings do. Creeping light. Your body
shifting in the slippage from dark to awake without

purpose, finding its way out the door because let's consider
for a moment that things begin with curious particles,
with proximity, and say a proper beginning

doesn't have to come headlong, fast and loud, say it's all
a matter of willingness, but then, what do I know? An animal
only sometimes upright, I drink the milk

directly from the carton, the peanut butter I eat
straight from the jar. I find satisfaction in licking the spoon, swiping it
back down for more. Intimacies most common, most coarse,

this is what I chase, but I can savor, too,
this elegance here: the hesitant day rising,
the colors, heaven's hemline frayed and dragging

across our floorboard. So much
loneliness but also, wonder. Dear world,
whatever you want, you only need ask this way,

and I will try to be generous.

Fantasy of Customer Service as Seduction

When called to cut from half a wheel of Gouda
or shear the nose from an eighth of Gruyère,
I carry the mammoth moons one handed
because I like to show off. We cut to order.
I siren-smile, holding the foot-long blade aloft,
and the customer might hesitate in this moment, *what if—*
gravity will do the bulk of the work, it's the angle
of the knife that determines what wedge I'll get: the grace
of a straight line from human hands. Perched
on my toes, arching my whole torso over the cheese
while flattening my left palm on the steel's spine and cupping
my right hand in an easy fist around the bolster.
Like holding a bat, like giving a hand job: ready
and ready to let go. Aggressive. Supplicant.

Rabbit Pâté

It arrived this afternoon, swaddled in plastic wrap
and packed in ice, already beheaded and defurred,
lustrous. The metal countertop beneath her

sanitized and gleaming, and thus readied, a chef
takes the animal apart, parting limbs from torso
with practiced hands and a paring knife, shearing

muscle loose from bone, his wrist loosening tissue
with swift flicks. His frame mounts a shadow
over the once-a-rabbit, the getting comes

easy, practiced travel through the memory grove:
brain to bicep to wrist to knife's edge. He stills,
holds the heart a beat. This heart, a rough nugget

of muscle, the size of a walnut. How much panting
this knot has wrought, the unseen leaps
it has propelled. He pinches. A small bubble of blood

hiccups out, drips down his thumb. Stroke
after stroke, history is flayed into filament. The life spent
in some unseen wood or brush—now just Bordeaux

bits on the cutting board. A man with large hands,
a parcel of meat, parceled out into usable
and refuse. Later, added fat and aromatics,

the food mill's burr and oven's heat. You'll never
taste the final clench, those last breaths
of bad luck. All the usual business, this is the way,

                                 the way it goes.

August Song of Flight

You unshuckable masterpiece of conviction and collapse, I shiver
in the light of your particular eclipse. You have a way
of pickling my tongue and rubbing out all my best-
learned lessons: now is when I walk away, now is when
I knit my lips together and keep myself clothed, oh,
but the plummy succor of your mouth
and the fractured shadow of your breath
raking hesitation from my limbs: here is how
I ruin in a field and flatten the cornstalks. Madman, you call
the full force of my attention into your palms that follow
the swoon of my jaw. I am a foolish animal. I should burn
for this. I do. For mischief and skin and the sight
of the night's bruised submission to morning. How much
of what I lie down with do I take with me when I rise?

Into the Woods

Fickle and full of feeling, the moon
in his eyes when he warns me,

I am trouble. Trouble does not say
sorry, *is this ok*, so often, but trouble

does wait until you are naked
to tell you there is a someone waiting

at home for him. I am in the wrong story.
Sorry, is this ok? I say, *yes*, I say,

*do not blow up a life for some
stolen moments.* I nearly do

mean it, I kiss it true. Swimming
in the same early midlife

unease: do we disappoint
our parents? Will we become them?

We do not use a condom as if to say
I dare you. I know we will

make nothing but the morning
come faster. All the things

I will only remember, *for now*—
not shelter or skin, nothing

I can live inside of. I kiss us
forgetful, I do it ruefully, as light

leaks into the borrowed room.

Origin Story: I

I am from the 134 and the twenty minutes or more
it takes to get anywhere. From sequins
and smiles spit shined and more than enough
but not enough to kickstart a solo
career. From I got mine and still, I wanted
yours, too. The greenest lawns and the hottest
summers that give the bougainvillea
her gorgeous hustle, her feathered grin
as she saunters across porches and chimneys
and cracked garage doors. I hail from impossible
water and the dreams that don't come
true or back or leave you with a cup
between lanes. I am from *there but for
the grace of God go I* and *it's just not
that hard to work harder.* I am from falling
asleep in my mother's station wagon as
as it flutters the last inch west
to the beach. So desperate to stay awake, to hear
the next song on the radio. I am from *sweet baby*
sing-alongs that outstrip even the golden
state's sunshine. I am from the hot feelings
my mother suggested might ruin me the way
they ruined her, so I kept meticulous record
of the fires I started. Pages and pages
and even pictures still bound and smoking
in the locked trunk where I left my honey.
I lost the key years ago.

Telling the Truth

July is fully fledged, has fully cleared
her throat. Her wet breath on me
in the morning, the sheets at my ankles and any
sense of the hour unfastened by the tricky
glitter of the light. What a beast summer
makes of me. I shimmy loose my clothes, beach
my body in strange beds, and it's no good,
I am thirsty, I am hungry, I am both
an unfocused appetite with legs
roaming through another supine
fever dream, and all the while,
the purple larkspur is in the meadow

unflinching. A weed, yes, but flowering,
birthed by heat, and a rogue wind
or two, the larkspur speckles the fields
left untended, swallows the governed
path. The purple denotes first love,
forgiving dispositions, but no, no novice
here, she is more stalk than petal,
hen of the yard, oh, virago
of my view, tell me how you came
into your ravishing, your fierce reach. Substitute
green for the need, substitute the flower
for the audacity of it, I say I want to be loved,
but what I mean is I want to understand power.

Consent

As if you could dig it up like a carrot
or shake it loose from the branches.

As if you could thwack it in half
like a coconut, could drink the milk

sloshing inside and be revived, as if you could command it
onto your tongue, as if it had a taste,

as if it could be poured or caught or captured or held
or worried loose like a tooth, a knot, a nail, as if it were an eye

fixed on a snake bisecting the path.
As if it could be summoned and hooded,

cut and partitioned: this: meat. This: poison. Many times

there was only the bright smell of gin
on my mouth and the butterscotch glow

of stupid I must have been haloed in, the sudden
seizure of my bitter orange and juniper tongue. Desire,

yes, also, urgency. But I could be
caught, I could be lightning

directed, flash inanimate. Out beyond
these walls, a ferocious wind

makes love to the trees in a yard,
pine needles scattering all over

the green, green ground. I want to say
I never assented to any role I was not fully certain I could sell,

but I, too, am susceptible to the suspicion I should be
dumb and grateful, like a cow or a potted plant.

Fantasy of Meaning More Than I Do

He side-smiled *uh-huh* to all I ever said and when
we found each other in the parking lot under a July moon—
Kismet, he said—it led where it always leads. Which is *yes*,
then nowhere. The lipstick came next. Suddenly, I'm saying
"Heat Wave" to the women who ask for the name
of my new act. They're getting a kick out of this. The ladies
who lunch love my bravado, and it's "Geranium"
to the yahoos and "Cherry Bomb" for the snobs
and the tourists who bike in from further flung, and this one man
sneers at "Cat's Tongue," *well, that's happening*. They don't know
it takes more muscle to get it off than keep it on, a fat smear
of cream rubbed hard into the crevices and the nook
where my upper lip binds with the lower and still, a stain
accrues. I continue exhaling in shades of rare. You forget
the order of things and you'll hear about it—
you have to be meticulous; you have to pay attention.

Graphic

I want to take up butchery. I want to write hot, dark books of the body,
lush with skunk smells, of nervousness and the rarely washed bits.
Abandoned cabbage, curdled milk—language stained with bile. I would feature

the yeasty tang of underwear freshly skimmed from the pelvis,
work in the foul heat of old corned beef. I would consider placing
a fresh carcass onto the poem's concrete floor. Manhandling prosciutto,

I often forget to treat it as flesh. Topographical map: New Mexico.
I think: pigments of summer. Not muscle wrung of blood, not the bullet
in the once-a-pig's skull and the dismembering that happened next. I've heard

the rectal tendons, bung, are sometimes sold as fake calamari. It's tricky
to get the smell out they say, but fry anything long enough and salt it
hard enough, it'll pass as a meal. One steel spike, one shot

violence is rendered edible. I know the weight of pork shoulder, pork haunch,
have heralded it above my head, pushed it across whirring blades
and layered sheer strips of it across waxed paper to sell. I've draped it

over luscious figs and roasted it crisp, praised the mouthfeel, its meaty
sweetness. What once trembled, was then still and soaking
in its own blood, is now polite, beautified. Consumable. A bigger knife then,

for poems that would make you cough, choke on what your tongue
has led you to forget. You would not flinch; you would not be able to get the odor
out of the back of your throat, you'd have to burn your clothes.

I Run Down All the Roads

The trees are dressed darker now for fall, but the leaves—
luminescent. Seurat mobiles of honey and rum nodding at me

as I run down the road ahead of you, not sweating yet, not breathing
heavy yet. I am chasing everything coming next: flowers

on the table. Our table? Your mother seems skeptical and your father
nonetheless charmed. I'm good with parents, all the parents, will we be

dinner party people? I eat standing up—will you want to sit
away from the TV? With napkins and plates and not with our hands—will you

start seeking out recipes? Put cutouts from *Food & Wine*
on the fridge and learn to use a mandoline? Can you learn, too,

to rise early as I do? I'm not optimistic. You snooze, you snooze several times,
pull me back, but I need the sight of the trees in this half light—you didn't believe

I would get up in the dark, they never do—you'll be asleep for hours, you were
dreaming restlessly, coughing, and turning in your sleep, are you

allergic to the sheets? Are you allergic to anything? The goldenrod
in a riot at the fence? Will we be observing cocktail hour? You must have

specific expectations. I go into every *maybe this time* already ahead
of the story, which is real, or not real, is as real as the fog now

blurring the view ahead, but you must still see me, I'm just a few yards
past, if you were beside me, were you to trace your fingers along the side

of my face your nails would come away dry, but soon, so soon my hairline
will be slick and were you to push the flat of your hand against my chest you would

feel a heart out of room, but I keep going, past the oaks, through
the vines, can I live through this? Can I circle back? Unhooked from facts, I run,

I run faster, you snore, I leap over that, I run down the future, I am so fast,
I chase down would you want to, I pant, I pant, I cannot be caught, I am not

being chased, it will never be as good as this. Silence. Eating alone.

Fantasy of Meaning What I Say

Let's put on a show, let's hold our own
revival, and on a narrow dirt tract of road
hardly traveled and nearly never at night,
we make a scene that would summon an anguished
Amen from my mother and thrill the hell
out of my younger self. Smell of dry bark,
smell of fistful of hair. A flick of my wrist
for a few of yours, the slightest friction, and there
goes the neighborhood. Have I ever loved
a wide sky? The way it kisses the dying grass
so tenderly. Everyone knows this story: wild child
pinned early to the pews pries out every nail
to stand. Smell of smoke, smell of something old
coming down. My value in the world has been
dependent on what I could avoid, what I could bring
together with effort and a song. You seem to know
I can ruin as well as I can solve. Loving
men had to be a better bet than waiting
on Him. Girlish fool. But I can have you
and the hot swoop of air leaving
your throat. You get exactly what you want,
and I get away with pretending all I ever wanted
was to give you what you want. I am the perfect
creature of belief, crying out not in confession
but in relief, the fall is all that's left, the ground,
the ground, surely the world can be remade
with salt and skin and hours taken from the same clock
begging us back to our rightful places
where you are trouble, and I am too good.

Getaway

It's just past sundown and Jess picks me up from the airport in a truck
she borrowed from a friend, and we drive straight to the French Quarter
because we're going out, we're getting hurricane drunk, we're toasting our shiny,
single selves with Jell-O-bright slurries, we intend to get soaked through
in another subtropical thunderstorm. The streets are already full
by the time we park, music and tourists spilling out of every open door.
We get our first drinks, and a bachelorette party hollers *come dance*
and of course we do: all of us holding hands, all of us grinning
before we are drinks again, off again; our off-kilter glee will not stay put,
it wants to walk us round and round, past every topless bar and neon
threshold and closed park and Everyone! Is saying! Hello! We sway past
Faulkner's old rooming house and the statue of Jesus Tennessee
used to visit. Jess says he says he was not religious, but it gave him comfort
to visit Jesus like this. The Christ is backlit for the night, his shadow consuming
the church's edifice. I believed once but I no longer see
what Tennessee saw and we move on, Jess's hand in mine, to the hotel
with the carousel bar, where you can drink in circles, the bartenders
staying put while you revolve. A handsome man wants to treat us, insists
I have a gin fizz, tells the bartender what I want before I can ask
for a Sazerac, because I am just that basic and because I want the thing
everyone says you are supposed to have and especially because I want bitter
and flowers, I want to give my eyes some Southern charm—but a gin fizz it is,
and it is all sugar and foam, and it tastes dystonic and wrong, as if I had
slipped into the Mississippi and the water tasted not like grit
but taffy. Vanilla. I smile, though—I am nothing if not eager
to be pleasing. I let the tall man stroke the tendons on the underside
of my wrist because I am wearing red tonight, because I am wearing the tall shoes
tonight, and perhaps, we'll kiss urgently like people do and *perhaps*
litters the air but Jess is putting her own cash down and pulling me out

and I think this is best, yes, almost certain because who knows
what can happen to an eager wrist, all that golden blood
thrumming *go* and this, this is how we get away.

Fantasy of Drinking Deep Enough

Alternately, you never call. You never apologize.
I walk myself home, inside, back to my car,
I put my shoes on, I only wear one, fuck my shoes—
you yell after me, I turn around, I don't,
I write you an email, a letter, I call, I don't,
I rip it all up, I flick matches and make small,
pitiful trash fires. Do I ever think
you made a mistake? I don't. I do. I don't,
mostly. I regret you; I miss you, I think about you
almost all the time, the way you touched
my stomach and said it was soft, and you said it
in such a nice way. I think about you leaving
notes all over the house telling me how lovely
you thought I was, what we needed to get
from the store, would I please find you
upstairs and kiss you because you missed me
already. Bring coffee. Bring an appetite. Do you
remember when I held your face with both hands
as I asked you, could we please do that
again? I do. I am in bed, I am in the road,
I am at my desk pulling you up from the well
with both hands. Here in the dark, you taste
so sweet, so much like pink
at the end of a blue day.

Modern Love

Without much preamble you declare you're going
to take me home with you, and without much
hesitation I agree, and before too long, we have
an understanding that lets us tumble easily
through the cold season. We do not agree
on much more than what can be had
at the hands of each other. What comes
next? I cannot speak to that. I've always been
a terrible liar. All the darker bits I've kept
sequestered, lurking at the corners
of my mouth. I double dip. I still follow
my exes. Littering. The car I left scraped up
in the parking lot, no note. There, too,
are the bigger slips—the girl in college
whose name I smeared, she slept around. I didn't
think of sluts the same way then, but also, too, there is
my general tendency to be self-righteous, to hike it
to the moral high ground first chance I get.
There is the best friend whose boyfriend I kissed, whose boyfriend
I let leave her for me, and the many,
many times I have taunted my parents that maybe
it's all their fault I am the mess I am, the lonely drunk
beside you now. There is not a sorrow hidden
I could solve, least of all yours. Least
of all mine. Perhaps we just lie here,
still as felled logs. We'll grow moss, and the sheets
beneath us will feather into dust. Mushrooms
will sprout between our toes, and we will never

say another word. What will have we made
in this bed? My nakedness and yours. I want
to believe there is some good in holding
and being held, in keeping some things to myself.

What We Take When We Stay

I am not shiny today. Rusty
like a rotten faucet spotting the water
in the glass. You mean to drink
deeply. You mean for me to feel
what you feel, a kind of fullness
of luck and so happy, happy is the word
you use, for our pairing. You're done,
and my dumb heart brayed for this, someone
with the answers to the crossword. Before
you fall asleep, you sigh yourself
into the soft den of my neck. The forgiving
gully receives while I begin
to resist the sheets. You're so close
and my dread is so intimate. Once when
my mother was a little girl, youngest of four,
she was obliged to play any game
proposed by her older brothers.
Hide and seek, one afternoon,
and she cleverly folded herself into the cabinet
under the sink, which had a hinge
to lock it, to keep the cat out
of the trash. Her brothers cleverly
latched it shut and left her there
even as she gave herself away, screaming
let me out. I imagine my mother—
who'll kick off a heavy blanket and hold
open the closet door while she pulls a sweater
from its hanger—ripping the seams
of her voice, trying to inspire

sympathy. There are no bolts
on our doors, but I swallowed her alarm
wholesale, like a snake swallows
a vole. If you lay head down
on my belly, you'll hear it moving.

How Different

He likes to pay but he likes it, too,
when I am loose, and while my wallet waits
on the table with the rest for the waiter to return,
he plucks mine up, brandishes my license, he cannot get enough

of this magic trick. *Look how different she looks, isn't it crazy?*
My friend and his wife, full bellied and content, smile
as my boyfriend pulls it back, staring at it, staring
at me. He has only known me short haired and winsome,

but here I am, preserved: dirty hair and a jaw
that could cut glass, he asks aloud, again, *what is it*
that makes you seem so different now? I can't quite—
I cut my hair and I gained thirty pounds, and I left

California and the man holding my purse
while I took that picture, holding my hand before that
in line, always holding me too close, it hurt,
but then, everything hurt then, and he,

this man now, who only knows me full
and softer to the touch, can't know. What I burned down,
what I built up to be here. There is no easy
song for it, nothing for a dinner table,

but he is human to wonder. I understand.
It's not unkindness that makes him ask, he doesn't know
this woman under plastic crowned with the bear
of the Golden State and backdropped in blue, wide eyed,

starving. He drapes his arm over my shoulder
that holds him up and tells me
and all our friends he thinks
I look happier now.

Fantasy of Accurate Expectations

First awake in early light with your head on his chest,
you consider the spare sheets you designated curtains
do not well diminish the eager flush of late summer
in your bedroom, where you know your way around,
dark or morning, but he does not. Strangeness
has slipped in—but not quite: strangeness knocked
politely, and not accustomed to saying no, you opened
the door and gave a welcome. His bearlike torso,
man, and animal at once, breathes your skull up
then down, and in this moment, you may have slipped
yourself, out of arbitration and second-guessing and through
a hatch, where you wait, sorry-grateful, and where the trees
have no color words have use for: the time Heaven
is said to tick. There will be times you go through
the gate and *flowers*. Other times not.

On Never Expecting My Reflection

Like a starfish, I grew back a whole body
from one lost limb. Skin screeching away from itself
to accommodate more of itself, from ribs to hips
a squall of stretch marks as every right angle capitulated
to poundage and the remand to remain upright and alive,
full and grateful, the duty clanging every hour
on the hour, cuckoo clock of wellness. I was promised
there was lovely country on the other side
of the crowded plates, all the goddamn shakes. You said
there would be grass so fleshy and smooth even I would succumb
to being held, the air so ripe it would fix
every bloom into open palms. I imagined gardenias
forgiving their stems and the weight of their fat, gorgeous
scent settling on me like a holy suit. I could have anticipated
there is no such place, no you, even, to sit with me
in this sulky dusk, shuddering at the shrill gobble
of the wild turkeys pecking the yard clean. Such appetites.
Ungovernable. I haven't stopped fantasizing
about giving it all back, carving myself down
like one of these birds roasted crisp,
but having arrived in the country of soft enough
to stop being saved, I get dressed instead.

In Praise Of—

We're discussing syntax in Wharton and James, and my mentor
is dropping the word *pleasure* like quarters into a parking meter,
is saying *pleasure* with this casual satisfaction, this deft ease
I associate with him and so, yes, I am listening, but I am also
having difficulty smoothing the rhythm in my wrists
and chest, feeling as though I should be turning around
to fend off the starched Puritans ever at my back,
ever ready to guard against stealth attacks on what
they believe to be their rightful territory: namely everything, namely
the full reach of my mind and all that it may draw itself toward, the word
pleasure flitting around like so many loose dandelion fronds after one blows
the head off the weed with a wish, no more remarkable
than finding a warm twenty in the pocket of a pair of jeans
after you've pulled them from the dryer. *Pleasure*. The word
offers, then, a particular illicit trill of sensation, suggests to memory
the most fat-tongued of feelings. The grass licking your ankles
as you skirt the high reeds making your way—easy,
slow—toward the water after months spent cramped, sweating
in boots. Warm bread, butter melting on it, reading D. H. Lawrence's
fruit poems and marveling, blushing, yes, admit it, that a thicket
of words could produce such—but then, pleasure
is reserved for that which brings satisfaction, not glee
or rapture but what first makes your mouth
open and round and encourages the skin
around your mouth to pull back and lifts up
your ears, the infinitely small moments before you bare
your teeth in a smile—the aromatic sheen
of gin on the olive at the bottom of an empty drink, the salt

and perfume and indehiscent bite a lovely, final
coda to the time you spent slowly taking
one swallow after another, savoring each word.

Lady Brett Ashley

Let the rest of them bake
in the sunshine and ennui:

the lady is the only one I want
to drink with. Not nearly

enough of her there—the lovely
curtain of her, breezing in then,

abandoned. But what a spirited
drunk she is, wearing her felt hat

with great aplomb and kissing hapless
young men in cabs. She stays

for the bullfight. Secretly
relishes it, I think. The color rising

in her, the blood just there, under
her skin. It seems impossible

for a woman to live without
a little fiction, so many men intent

on muscling their way to the end
of the sentence. The room

falls away as I aim to catch
her gimlet eye, she misses

                          nothing.

What Is Gold

Brick is the color of the trunk
lifting each sequined limb aloft,
and brilliant is the color of the leaves
seen shimmering from the bed
where you are taking me apart.

I would have you bury me
under your tongue. How often
I wept in girlhood for unclaimed desires.
The high, myopic whine
in the word itself was intimate

to me. What I've learned to keep to myself
is little, ever so inclined to skin
myself open like a ripe orange. I trouble
with good things, cannot let them
just be. Like you, with your

faithful mouth. Look at me
here, splayed out in the back half
of the bloom, fizzing
with pleasure, pleasure
scurrying through the skin

like rats on fire. I would say
I want you, but the truth is hotter, worse,
is running for its life, every miserable
nerve swimming down with the same
worry-bomb: I'd rather miss you.

From your spring-sweet mouth
to my barbed mind, here at the edge
of all our greenery, would you always
want a body so pliant? So tenuous?
You say you can stay, say you're going
to for as long as I let you.

Season of No Answer

You kiss me with your mouth open, like the world
is certain and spring will always rise up

to meet you, as though the flowers themselves
will never-not open in your direction, will forever

tilt their heads back to gulp the rain down in green
fistfuls while the dirt is wet and pleased. You tell me

you have no doubts and that I should be capable
of some surety at this point. I watch the water

fall into the ground. Were you more
godly, you would spit me out.

Who Can Say

On the back patio are the mothers free of children, holding court
and also full glasses of wine and gesticulating to their concordant
frustrations: the decline of one's breasts, stretch marks, yes,

but also, too, those rough, first months of miraculous exhaustion
that were still haloed with an ineffable, painful kind
of wonder. This is when I leave them for the other women

smoking at the fence on the outer rim of the lawn, where I am
offered my own, already lit. We are quiet until I am asked
about a new job and another about her mother

who is beginning to forget where the milk goes. We don't speak
of the "not now" or "not ever" or "only under these conditions" or perhaps
not alone or when enough has been saved and so on, and when later,

one of the mothers finds me, says she is sorry for making me leave,
her apology seems more admonishment than grace. She wants, I think,
to tell me it's my failing, the way I flinched, that I should

be proud of them. I say, "I needed more wine," "I needed to pee," "I'm sorry,"
and I cut around her and the fence and out toward the lake,
only stopping short at cluster of geese roosting. How to articulate

the confusion and rift, their echo-pain a figment of a wish
I do not know how to enact or chance or even assign language to, let alone admit, yes,
to hold in my own arms a body I received, watered? Indefinite and forever

love incarnate? I can only stand to be in love for days at a time.
What say you, clouds, to the querulous posture of these geese? The rich scent
of their fresh shit wafting up from the muck, their malevolent hissing

if one comes too close. What kind of invitation did I expect?
The new-green reeds shivering across the water
don't care if I witness their tremulous movements.

This tight circle of my life. I have been intent to wish for less,
and what has this restraint cost, what has been left uncalled for?
I do not know what I would say to sons, but I would tell daughters,

may you have the dumb blunt will of a tank.
May you have pulpy hearts and sturdy frames.
May your loyalty never get the best of you. May you take down kingdoms.

May you hold your grasp, may you get more than you deserve.
May you wind someone else's pleasure
round your finger. May you feel no shame for getting yours.

May your mind carbonate
                    at the sight of green leaves.

Again, Again

Not like a tap turned on and not like a match struck
and certainly not like flicking on a light. It is not sudden.

It is barely sweet. Ripe? Hard to tell. Fingers
pressed carefully into the skin, imagine say, a pear,

green, faintly so, and tenuous, as though the green
were a blush, as though the pear at the prospect

of being plucked from its tree so many weeks ago
flushed a shade that recalls grass dying in the fall

or the barest beginnings of scallion stems.
Sometimes you tell the story in fits, sometimes

one line at a time.

Fantasy of Loving the Fantasy

My tongue fingers the pit
of the olive at the bottom of the third
martini. I am folding his laundry
like I like it, and I almost do,
this well-worn gesture
newly applied. Playing house.
I almost love it, the clamor
and mess he makes for dinner,
how he dirties every pot
and lid. How often

I have practiced for this
domestic position: my posture
nearly perfect, my concerns
inscrutable. My sharp-toothed self
now well petted and settled,
no longer stalking the birds,
not lingering near the back
door. Which is not locked.
I had a habit once, you know,
of accidentally setting things on fire.
A bagel that caught in the toaster
and swept a fiery lick up the cabinet
over the stove. The patio table
with a spectacular crater left in it
from the citronella torch I tipped
askew on my way to the pool. There were,
too, of course, the multiple times

I have left a candle burning,
poured oil in the cast iron
when it's still too hot. I have
a habit of believing myself

impenetrable. It was never
on purpose, I say
about the fires, I am just
so clumsy. Can you hear my laugh
as I say it? You must know
I lingered there, in the caustic
luster of them, thought carefully
of letting them go.

Mirror, Mirror

I wear the long sentence like a fur, like a silk slip
rivering from shoulder to knee, my trouble
tongue eludes the dam. Apple of no one's eye,
I am a sour-flecked June, the plum knot
of color punishing the horizon line,
and lest you forget these are notes for a story
in which I am not my mother, I am in the swell
of sulfur singing up from the brackish water
running toward the woods where the dark
strokes the skin of trees and gold-eyed animals
whisper in anticipation of their dinner. She has not visited
in years. I scared her off early, every flash of her own
mother in me—wild, unyielding—unsettling
the agreement we have where she gets the bricks,
and I get to be the wolf. I say she is scared,
but I have skirted the issue. I should say that I am afraid
of her fence. With juice and grammar, I have eluded
every gate, save the one where I talk myself out
of her reflection. My mother, the good
woman, faithful woman, who reminds me I am so lucky
you are so good to me. Look at me, preparing
a meal for your eager mouth—you are nothing
if not grateful, and here I am doing just as I said
I wouldn't, lighting the candles and sitting
quietly on my hands.

Nothing Is in the Yard but the Dark

As if on a raft, I lean back
into the swelling dark,
the air behind me thick
with pollen and riven with leaf-light
from the sun, which is nearly
down. Just me and the lawn,
no fence, a woman and her plot
of land. Do we need a whole house?
All the boxes? In the land
of what might have been, I call you
and ask you not to come back.
I use a pet name, you don't laugh.
Your laugh—in this dream I knew
years ago, what I was looking for. I sign
my emails "yours" when I am all
but. Second thoughts? No. Just lights
flickering in a closed room. A slow leak
in a hot air balloon. Just grace. The grass
is coming up high in the yard. I wait outside
in the nearly-night and try to remember
how to howl.

May

Goose shit and babies, weddings
and asparagus, so much green,
so much flowering and shearing
in this season, your body hardly belongs
to you. It is pink. Damp. Up to your knees
in sweat and tomatoes, rummaging
your hands through the dirt,
testing its softness, how it might receive
what you might press in. Radishes, say.
Something bitter that can be coaxed
into loveliness with butter,
lots of salt. Does anyone
miss their sweaters? The wind
making a new face of your face?
I do. Don't tell. I flinch
in the light of renewal.
Would that the world would let me grow
alone, would that the season could be
reduced to the duration of an apricot.

I esteem that fruit's coy arrival,
its rusty sugar, wildflowers
and bark, rustling the tongue
like a mouthful of monarchs, like a fistful
of marigold petals and the gusts
that wrested them loose. How little
an apricot cares for my affection. Held
too eagerly: collapse. Even if
I am measured in my devouring, all too fast

the pit. Rough and furrowed,
like old teeth, why can't
I trust what can be kept? I lap up
the juice left in my palm,
throw away the stone.

Notes

"Fantasy of Losing My Suburban Cool" lifts/rifts on a line from Anton Chekhov's *The Seagull*: Act II, Trigorin, to Nina: ". . . Then a man comes along, sees her, and ruins her life because he has nothing better to do. Destroys her like this seagull here."

A prize for anyone who can catch every inflection and sentiment indebted to Stephen Sondheim, but a few direct references that require proper attribution include:

"Into the Woods" lifts the line "I am in the wrong story" from Sondheim's musical of the same name.

"Fantasy of Accurate Expectations" employs the compound adjective "sorry-grateful" from the musical *Company*.

"Origin Story: I" takes its form from George Ella Lyon's "Where I'm From" poem.

"Into the Woods" also mentions stolen moments, a call out to Kim Addonizio's poem "Stolen Moments" from her collection *What Is This Thing Called Love*.

In "Graphic," the speaker expresses a desire to write, ". . . hot, dark books of the body," a direct theft from Tony Hoagland's review of Addonizio's aforementioned collection.

"In Praise Of—" wishes to thank the A. E. Stallings poem "Olives," from her collection of the same name, for an introduction to the word "indehiscent."

"Lady Brett Ashley" means to summon Lady Brett Ashley from *The Sun Also Rises* by Ernest Hemingway.

"What Is Gold" is in conversation with Robert Frost's "Nothing Gold Can Stay."

Acknowledgments

Grateful acknowledgement is made to the editors and readers of the following journals where these poems originally appeared, sometimes in earlier forms.

The Boiler	"August Song of Flight" "Fantasy of Losing My Suburban Cool"
Four Way Review	"Consent"
Kenyon Review	"May"
Moist Poetry Journal	"What Is Gold"
Nashville Review	"Fantasy of Loving the Fantasy" "How Different"
Painted Bride Quarterly	"Rabbit Pâté"
ROARfeminist.org	"In Praise Of—" "Who Can Say"
Southern Indiana Review	"Mirror, Mirror"
SWWIM Every Day	"Again, Again"

Buckets of gratitude—

To the Warren Wilson MFA Program for Writers, which was the making of me, and to my supervisors/mentors during my time there, Connie Voisine & Jennifer Grotz & Daniel Tobin & Ellen Bryant Voigt, for bringing me into a communion my own mind, and to James Longenbach, in particular, who first demonstrated the thrill of making good English sentences. His ferocious intellect and wit and unyielding decency of spirit were transformative. He is dearly missed.

To Friends of Writers and the support they offered me during my time at Warren Wilson. To Dorianne Laux, for seeing something in this manuscript's early days and awarding me the Levis Prize through FOW.

To the Bread Loaf Writers' Conference and Michael Collier & Jennifer Grotz's stewardship of it in the years since I first arrived. The world was wider after my time there. For my workshop teachers there, Sally Keith & C. Dale Young & Vievee Francis & francine j. harris, who never flinched when saying what needed to be said and did so with more grace than I could ever deserve.

To Martha Rhodes, for inviting me to The Frost Place initially and to the place itself, for being so magical. To Gabrielle Calvocoressi & Maudelle Driskell, for making it especially so, and to Sandra Lim, for being a such a thoughtful teacher.

To Han VanderHart & Benjamín García, for being catty and smart in the right proportions.

To Caroline Mar & Nathan McClain & Michael Jarmer for being the first readers of this manuscript. Your feedback was gold.

To Noah Stetzer, for deer sightings, dead and otherwise; Ross White, for the necessary bullying and the editorial insight. This book would have no spine without either of you. To Alana Dunn, for clarity of vision. To Maia Flore, for articulating in a cover image what the book could not.

To my Wally cadre, Abigail Cahill & Katherine Rooks & Rose Skelton & Nomi Stone & Kate Murr & Ashley McIlwain Nissler & Emile Beck & Margaret Draft, for coming to the table with me so, so many times to feast and debate. To Rebecca Friedman & Faith Holsaert & Jennifer Leah Büchi & Robin Rosen Chang, for company on Tuesday nights. To Tracy Winn, for keeping the faith.

To Ellen Bush, Jessica O'Dell, Barbara Patrachek, Daniel Simone, Cristina Jonson, and my whole wild run club family, for keeping me out and about and moving in the world.

To my dear Boston-based babes, Caroline Beimford & Caitlin McGill & Sara Freeman, upon whose fellowship I depend.

To Eric, who is too much and is still, somehow, just right.

And to my parents and stepparents and siblings, who tolerated my ungovernable fountain of speech and fits of feeling from the start. Thank you for not giving up and throwing me in a river. Dad, my favorite second act, the next book is yours.

About the Author

Jennifer Funk is a native Californian trying to prove her mettle in New England. A graduate of Bennington College and of Warren Wilson's MFA Program for Writers, she has been a scholarship recipient of the Bread Loaf Writers' Conference and The Frost Place. Her poems have appeared in *Kenyon Review*, *Four Way Review*, *Cimarron Review*, *The Boiler*, and elsewhere. This is her first collection.